Lorraine Turner

barbecues & salads

simple and delicious easy-to-make recipes

This is a Parragon Publishing Book
This edition published in 2005

Parragon Publishing
Queen Street House
4 Queen Street
Bath, BA1 1HE, UK

Copyright © Exclusive Editions 2002

ISBN: 1–40543–864–9

Printed in China

Produced by The Bridgewater Book Company Ltd

Photographer Calvey Taylor Haw
Home Economist Sara Hesketh

NOTES FOR THE READER

- This book uses imperial, metric, or US cup measurements. Follow the same units of measurement throughout; do not mix imperial and metric.

- All spoon measurements are level: teaspoons are assumed to be 5 ml, and tablespoons are assumed to be 15 ml.

- Unless otherwise stated, milk is assumed to be whole milk, eggs and individual vegetables such as potatoes are medium, and pepper is freshly ground black pepper.

- Recipes using raw or very lightly cooked eggs should be avoided by infants, the elderly, pregnant women, convalescents, and anyone suffering from an illness.

- The times given are an approximate guide only. Preparation times differ according to the techniques used by different people and the cooking times may also vary from those given. Optional ingredients, variations or serving suggestions have not been included in the calculations.

contents

introduction

There is something wonderfully evocative about the smell of grilled food: it can conjure up memories of lazy summer evenings on the beach, or delicious aromas wafting from an outdoor campfire. Grilling al fresco has never been easier, either: there is an ever-widening range of barbecue grills available nowadays, and with the advent of portable and disposable grills, this method of cooking food has become extremely easy, cheap, and quick.

Some barbecue grills use coals or hardwood, and others are electric. Always abide by the safety instructions that come with your grill, and be careful around naked flames and fuel. Keep children and pets away from the cooking area, and position your grill so that the smoke will not be a nuisance to other people.

chicken satay skewers with lime
page 16

spicy john dory
page 38

This book contains a delicious array of dishes, from sizzling poultry and meat and mouthwatering fish to an extravaganza of vegetarian meals and salads. To round everything off, there is also a stunning selection of quick and easy desserts. So whatever the occasion, whether you are traveling far from home or entertaining friends in your yard, there is something here to satisfy every appetite.

easy

Recipes are graded as follows:
1 spoon = easy;
2 spoons = very easy;
3 spoons = extremely easy.

serves 4

Recipes generally serve four people. Simply halve the ingredients to serve two, taking care not to mix imperial and metric measurements.

10 minutes

Preparation time. Where marinating, chilling, or cooling are involved, these times have been added on separately: eg, 15 minutes + 30 minutes to marinate.

10 minutes

Cooking time. Cooking times don't include the cooking of side dishes or accompaniments served with the main dishes.

avocado, corn & walnut salad
page 70

apple & melon kabobs
page 84

Grilling is a delicious way of cooking a variety of different meats and poultry, and an easy and satisfying way to prepare meals. The poultry and meat dishes in this chapter are all simple to prepare and quick to cook, and the sheer variety of accompanying ingredients and marinades ensures that there will always be an exciting assortment of flavorsome, mouthwatering dishes for your barbecue grill.

poultry & meat

spicy grilled chicken

very easy   serves 4

15 minutes   20–30
+ 2½ hours   minutes
to marinate

ingredients

MARINADE
1½ tbsp chili oil
½ tsp brown sugar
½ tsp salt
1½ tsp allspice
1½ tsp dried mixed herbs
pepper
1½ tsp grated fresh root ginger
4 shallots, chopped
6 scallions, trimmed and
   finely chopped

4 garlic cloves, chopped
1 green chili and 1 red chili, seeded

CHICKEN
4 skinless, boneless chicken breasts,
   cut into slices
juice of 3 limes
scant ⅔ cup water
wedges of fresh lime, to garnish
salad greens, to serve

Put the chili oil, sugar, salt, allspice, and mixed herbs into a food processor and season with plenty of pepper. Blend until combined.

Add the grated ginger, shallots, scallions, and garlic. Chop the chilies, add to the shallot mixture, and blend until fairly smooth. Transfer to a glass pitcher or bowl, cover with plastic wrap, and set aside.

Put the chicken slices into a nonmetallic (glass or ceramic) bowl, which will not react with acid. Pour over the lime juice and water, then add enough marinade to cover the chicken. Cover with plastic wrap and refrigerate for 2½ hours. Cover the remaining marinade with plastic wrap and refrigerate until the chicken is ready.

When the chicken slices are thoroughly marinated, lift them out and grill them over hot coals for 20–30 minutes, or until cooked right through, turning them frequently and basting with the remaining marinade. Serve on a bed of salad greens.

sweet & sour chicken wings

very easy   serves 4

5 minutes   20 minutes
+ 2½ hours
to marinate

ingredients

MARINADE
2 tbsp sweet sherry
3 tbsp sherry vinegar or red
 wine vinegar
4 tbsp soy sauce
scant ⅔ cup orange juice
scant ½ cup chicken bouillon or vegetable
 bouillon
¼ cup brown sugar
pepper
1 tbsp tomato paste

2 garlic cloves, finely chopped
1 red chili, seeded and finely chopped

CHICKEN
4 lb/1.8 kg chicken wings

GARNISH
wedges of orange
1 long, red chili, made into a flower
 (see below)

Put the sherry, vinegar, soy sauce, orange juice, bouillon, and sugar into a food processor and season well. Blend until combined. Add the tomato paste, garlic, and chili, and blend until smooth. Separate the chicken wings at the joints and put them into a nonmetallic (glass or ceramic) bowl, which will not react with acid. Pour over enough marinade to cover the chicken, cover with plastic wrap and refrigerate for 2½ hours. Cover the remaining marinade with plastic wrap and refrigerate until the chicken is ready.

When the chicken wings are thoroughly marinated, lift them out and grill them over hot coals for about 20 minutes, turning them frequently and basting with the remaining marinade. Cut into a thick part of a wing to check that the chicken is cooked all the way through. If it is still pink in the middle, continue to grill until the chicken is thoroughly cooked. Garnish with orange wedges and a chili flower (made by making ½-inch/1-cm slits in a chili and soaking in iced water for 30 minutes until fanned out.)

thai-style chicken chunks

very easy   serves 4

10 minutes   20 minutes
+ 2½ hours
to marinate

ingredients

MARINADE
1 red chili and 1 green chili,
    seeded and finely chopped
2 garlic cloves, chopped
1¾ oz/50 g chopped fresh cilantro
1 tbsp finely chopped fresh
    lemongrass
½ tsp ground turmeric
½ tsp garam masala
2 tsp brown sugar

2 tbsp fish sauce
1 tbsp lime juice
salt and pepper

CHICKEN
4 skinless, boneless chicken breasts,
    cut into small chunks
chopped fresh cilantro, to garnish
freshly cooked jasmine rice, to serve

Put the red and green chilies, garlic, cilantro, and lemongrass into a food processor and process until coarsely chopped. Add the turmeric, garam masala, sugar, fish sauce, and lime juice, season well, and blend until smooth.

Put the chicken chunks into a nonmetallic (glass or ceramic) bowl, which will not react with acid. Pour over enough marinade to cover the chicken, then cover with plastic wrap and refrigerate for at least 2½ hours. Cover the remaining marinade with plastic wrap and refrigerate until the chicken is ready.

When the chicken chunks are thoroughly marinated, lift them out and grill them over hot coals for 20 minutes or until cooked right through, turning them frequently and basting with the remaining marinade. Arrange the chicken on serving plates with some freshly cooked jasmine rice, garnish with chopped cilantro, and serve.

sherried chicken & mushroom kabobs

very easy   serves 4

15 minutes   15–20
+ 2½ hours   minutes
to marinate

ingredients

MARINADE

scant ¼ cup soy sauce
2 tbsp sweet sherry
scant ¼ cup vegetable oil
1 tsp brown sugar
1 tbsp honey
1 garlic clove, finely chopped
pepper

KABOBS

6 skinless, boneless chicken
　breasts, cubed
16 white mushrooms
16 pearl onions
16 cherry tomatoes
fresh flatleaf parsley, to garnish
freshly steamed or boiled rice, to serve

Put the soy sauce, sweet sherry, oil, sugar, and honey into a large bowl. Add the garlic and mix until well combined. Season with plenty of pepper.

Thread the chicken cubes onto 8 skewers, alternating them with the mushrooms, onions, and cherry tomatoes. When the skewers are full (leave a small space at either end), transfer them to the bowl and turn them in the sherry mixture until they are well coated. Cover with plastic wrap and place in the refrigerator to marinate for at least 2½ hours.

When the kabobs are thoroughly marinated, lift them out and grill them over hot coals for 15–20 minutes or until cooked right through, turning them frequently and basting with the remaining marinade. Arrange the kabobs on a bed of freshly cooked rice, garnish with fresh flatleaf parsley, and serve.

chicken satay skewers with lime

extremely
easy

serves 4

10 minutes
+ 2½ hours
to marinate

15 minutes

ingredients

MARINADE
scant ½ cup soy sauce
scant ½ cup lime juice
2 tbsp smooth peanut butter
2 tbsp garam masala
1 tbsp brown sugar
2 garlic cloves, finely chopped
1 small red chili, seeded and
   finely chopped
pepper

SKEWERS
6 skinless, boneless chicken
   breasts, cubed

GARNISH
fresh cilantro leaves, shredded
wedges of lime
freshly steamed or boiled rice, or crisp
   salad greens, to serve

Put the soy sauce, lime juice, peanut butter, garam masala, sugar, garlic, and chili into a large bowl and mix until well combined. Season with plenty of pepper.

Thread the chicken cubes onto skewers (leave a small space at either end). Transfer them to the bowl and turn them in the peanut butter mixture until they are well coated. Cover with plastic wrap and place in the refrigerator to marinate for at least 2½ hours.

When the skewers are thoroughly marinated, lift them out and grill them over hot coals for 15 minutes or until cooked right through, turning them frequently and basting with the remaining marinade. Arrange the skewers on a bed of freshly cooked rice or crisp salad greens, garnish with cilantro leaves and lime wedges, and serve.

tangy pork ribs

easy   serves 4

15 minutes   2½–2¾ hours

ingredients

1¼ tsp salt
2 tsp paprika
2 tsp pepper
3 lb/1.3 kg pork ribs
1 tbsp chili or vegetable oil
1 onion, finely chopped
6 scallions, trimmed and chopped
3 garlic cloves, chopped
2 tsp finely chopped fresh ginger root
1 red chili, chopped
1 tbsp chopped fresh cilantro

1 tbsp chopped flatleaf parsley
1 tbsp sweet sherry
1½ tbsp brown sugar
4 tbsp Chinese chili bean sauce
1 tbsp tomato paste
1 tbsp rice wine
1 tbsp sherry vinegar
scant ½ cup orange juice
2½ tbsp soy sauce
salt and pepper
wedges of orange, to serve

Preheat the oven to 475°F/240°C. Combine the salt, paprika, and pepper in a baking dish and then add the ribs. Turn them in the dish to coat them well all over. Cook in the center of the preheated oven for 1¾–2 hours, then remove the dish from the oven, lift out the ribs, drain off the fat, and set aside.

Heat the oil in a skillet. Add the onion, scallions, garlic, ginger, and chili, and stir-fry over a high heat for 1 minute. Then add the herbs, sherry, sugar, chili bean sauce, tomato paste, rice wine, vinegar, orange juice, and soy sauce. Stir in a large pinch of salt and season well with pepper. Bring to a boil, lower the heat, and simmer for 15–20 minutes, stirring occasionally.

To cook the ribs, coat them in the sauce, then grill them over hot coals for 7–10 minutes on each side, or until cooked right through, turning them frequently and basting with more sauce as necessary. Serve at once, accompanied by orange wedges.

curried lamb skewers

very easy   serves 4

20 minutes
+ 8 hours
to marinate

15 minutes

ingredients

MARINADE
2 tsp vegetable oil
1 tsp curry powder
1 tsp garam masala
2 tsp granulated sugar
scant ⅔ cup plain yogurt

SKEWERS
14 oz/400 g boneless lamb, cubed
5 oz/140 g dried apricot halves

1 red or green bell pepper, seeded and cut
    into small chunks
2 zucchini, cubed
16 pearl onions
fresh cilantro leaves, to garnish

TO SERVE
freshly steamed or boiled rice
crisp salad greens

Put the oil, spices, sugar, and yogurt into a large bowl and mix until well combined.

Thread the lamb onto 8 skewers, alternating it with the apricot halves, red or green bell pepper, zucchini, and onions. When the skewers are full (leave a small space at either end), transfer them to the bowl and turn them in the yogurt mixture until they are well coated. Cover with plastic wrap and place in the refrigerator to marinate for at least 8 hours or overnight.

When the skewers are thoroughly marinated, lift them out and grill them over hot coals, turning them frequently, for 15 minutes or until the meat is cooked right through. Serve with freshly cooked rice and crisp salad greens, garnished with fresh cilantro leaves.

thai-spiced beef & bell pepper kabobs

very easy   serves 4

20 minutes   10–15
+ 2½ hours   minutes
to marinate

ingredients

MARINADE
2 tbsp sherry
2 tbsp rice wine
scant ⅓ cup soy sauce
scant ⅓ cup hoisin sauce
3 cloves garlic, finely chopped
1 red chili, seeded and
    finely chopped
1½ tbsp grated fresh root ginger
3 scallions, trimmed and finely chopped

salt and pepper

KABOBS
2 lb 4 oz/1 kg loin end or short loin steak,
    cubed
2 large red bell peppers, seeded and cut
    into small chunks

green and red lettuce, to serve

Put the sherry, rice wine, soy sauce, hoisin sauce, garlic, chili, ginger, and scallions into a large bowl and mix until well combined. Season to taste.

Thread the meat onto 8 skewers, alternating it with chunks of red bell pepper. When the skewers are full (leave a small space at either end), transfer them to the bowl and turn them in the soy sauce mixture until they are well coated. Cover with plastic wrap and place in the refrigerator to marinate for 2½ hours or overnight.

When the skewers are thoroughly marinated, lift them out and grill them over hot coals, turning them frequently, for 10–15 minutes or until the meat is cooked right through. Serve at once on a bed of green and red lettuce.

greek-style beef kabobs

very easy

serves 4

25 minutes

15–20 minutes

ingredients

1 small onion, finely chopped
1 tbsp chopped fresh cilantro
large pinch of paprika
¼ tsp allspice
¼ tsp ground coriander
¼ tsp brown sugar
1 lb/450 g ground beef

salt and pepper
vegetable oil, for brushing
fresh cilantro leaves, to garnish

TO SERVE
freshly cooked bulgur wheat or rice
mixed salad

Put the onion, fresh cilantro, spices, sugar, and beef into a large bowl and mix until well combined.

On a clean counter, use your hands to shape the mixture into sausages around skewers. Brush them lightly with vegetable oil.

Grill the kabobs over hot coals, turning them frequently, for 15–20 minutes or until cooked right through. Arrange the kabobs on a platter of freshly cooked bulgur wheat or rice and garnish with fresh cilantro leaves. Serve with a mixed salad.

cherry tomato, ham & pineapple skewers

extremely easy

serves 4

10 minutes

10 minutes

ingredients

1 tbsp vegetable oil

1 tbsp white wine vinegar

1 tsp mustard powder

1 tbsp honey

1 lb/450 g cooked ham steak, cubed

1 lb/450 g canned pineapple chunks, drained

12 cherry tomatoes

freshly cooked rice, fresh salad greens, or crusty bread, to serve

Put the oil, vinegar, mustard powder, and honey into a bowl and mix until well combined.

Thread the ham onto skewers, alternating it with pineapple chunks and whole cherry tomatoes. When the skewers are full (leave a small space at either end), brush them with the honey mixture until they are well coated.

Grill the skewers over hot coals, turning them frequently, for about 10 minutes or until cooked right through. Serve them with freshly boiled rice, fresh salad greens, or crusty bread.

grilled pork sausages with thyme

very easy   serves 4

15 minutes   15 minutes
+ 45 minutes
to chill

ingredients

1 garlic clove, finely chopped
1 onion, grated
1 small red chili, seeded and
  finely chopped
1 lb/450 g lean ground pork
⅓ cup almonds, toasted
  and ground
1 cup fresh bread crumbs

1 tbsp finely chopped fresh thyme
salt and pepper
flour, for dusting
vegetable oil, for brushing

TO SERVE
fresh bread rolls
slices of onion, lightly cooked
tomato catsup and/or mustard

Put the garlic, onion, chili, pork, almonds, bread crumbs, and fresh thyme into a large bowl. Season well with salt and pepper and mix until well combined.

Using your hands, form the mixture into sausage shapes. Roll each sausage in a little flour, then transfer to a bowl, cover with plastic wrap, and refrigerate for 45 minutes.

Brush a piece of aluminum foil with oil, then put the sausages on the foil and brush them with a little more vegetable oil. Transfer the sausages and foil to the barbecue grill. Grill over hot coals, turning the sausages frequently, for about 15 minutes or until cooked right through. Serve with bread rolls, cooked sliced onion, and tomato catsup and/or mustard.

spicy thai-style burgers

very easy   serves 4

15 minutes   10–16 minutes

ingredients

scant ½ cup fresh bread crumbs, white or whole-wheat
1½ tbsp finely chopped scallions
1 garlic clove, finely chopped
1½ tbsp chopped fresh lemongrass
1½ tbsp chopped fresh cilantro
½ oz/15 g almonds, chopped
½ oz/15 g groundnuts, chopped
1 lb 2 oz/500 g ground beef

1 small red chili, seeded and finely chopped
salt and pepper

TO SERVE
wedges of lemon and lime
fresh shredded Napa cabbage
hamburger buns

Put the bread crumbs, scallions, garlic, lemongrass, cilantro, nuts, beef, and chili into a large bowl, and mix until well combined. Season with salt and pepper.

Using your hands, form the mixture into burger shapes. Grill the burgers over hot coals for 5–8 minutes on each side or until cooked right through. Serve in hamburger buns with wedges of lemon and lime, and shredded Napa cabbage.

beefburgers with chili & basil

very easy   serves 4

10 minutes   10–16 minutes

ingredients

1 lb 7 oz/650 g ground beef
1 red bell pepper, seeded and
   finely chopped
1 garlic clove, finely chopped
2 small red chilies, seeded and
   finely chopped
1 tbsp chopped fresh basil
½ tsp powdered cumin
salt and pepper

sprigs of fresh basil, to garnish
hamburger buns, to serve

Put the beef, red bell pepper, garlic, chilies, basil, and cumin into a bowl and mix until well combined. Season with salt and pepper.

Using your hands, form the mixture into burger shapes. Grill the burgers over hot coals for 5–8 minutes on each side or until cooked right through. Garnish with sprigs of basil and serve with hamburger buns.

Fish is a very healthy food: it is rich
in vitamins and minerals, and offers
a nutritious alternative to poultry and
meat. This chapter contains some
delicious recipes that you can easily
prepare and cook on a barbecue grill.
It rings the changes with a variety of
fresh fish including tuna, salmon,
and John Dory, and a wealth of
accompanying ingredients and flavors
from different parts of the world.

fish & seafood

grilled salmon

extremely easy

serves 4

5 minutes + 2 hours to marinate

20 minutes

MARINADE

scant ½ cup vegetable oil
scant ½ cup dry white wine
1 tbsp black molasses
1 tbsp brown sugar
1 tbsp soy sauce
1 garlic clove, chopped
pinch of allspice
salt and pepper

SALMON

4 salmon steaks, about 7 oz/200 g each
wedges of lemon, to garnish
crisp salad greens, to serve

Put the oil, wine, black molasses, sugar, soy sauce, garlic, and allspice into a large bowl, and mix until well combined. Season with salt and pepper.

Rinse the salmon steaks under cold running water, then pat dry with paper towels. Add them to the wine mixture and turn them until they are well coated. Cover with plastic wrap and place in the refrigerator to marinate for at least 2 hours or overnight.

When the steaks are thoroughly marinated, lift them out and grill them over hot coals for about 10 minutes on each side or until cooked right through, turning them frequently and basting with the remaining marinade. About halfway through the cooking time, add the lemon wedges and cook for 4–5 minutes, turning once. Arrange the steaks on a bed of fresh salad greens, garnish with the lemon wedges, and serve.

spicy john dory

very easy serves 4

15 minutes 15 minutes

ingredients

AIOLI
4 large garlic cloves, finely chopped
2 small egg yolks
scant 1 cup extra-virgin olive oil
2 tbsp lemon juice
1 tbsp Dijon mustard
1 tbsp chopped fresh tarragon
salt and pepper

JOHN DORY
2 John Dory, filleted

2 garlic cloves, chopped
2 shallots, grated
1 small red chili, seeded and chopped
1 tbsp lemon juice
wedges of lemon, to garnish

TO SERVE
crisp salad greens
raw and lightly blanched vegetables

To make the aioli, put the garlic and egg yolks into a food processor and process until well blended. With the motor running, slowly pour in the olive oil through the feeder tube until a thick mayonnaise forms. Add the lemon juice, mustard, tarragon, and seasoning, and blend until smooth. Transfer to a nonmetallic (glass or ceramic) bowl, which will not react with acid. Cover with plastic wrap and refrigerate until ready to serve.

Rinse the fish under cold running water, then pat dry with paper towels. In a separate bowl, mix together the garlic, shallots, chili, and lemon juice. Rub the shallot mixture onto both sides of the fillets, then grill them over hot coals for about 15 minutes or until cooked right through, turning them once. Arrange the steaks on a bed of crisp salad greens, garnish with lemon wedges, and serve separately with the aioli and the vegetables for dipping.

tuna & tarragon skewers

extremely
easy

serves 4

10 minutes
+ 30 minutes
to marinate

10 minutes

MARINADE

2 tbsp white wine

3 tbsp balsamic vinegar

1 tbsp extra-virgin olive oil

1 garlic clove, finely chopped

salt and pepper

SKEWERS

10 ½ oz/300 g fresh tuna steaks

1 lb/450 g white mushrooms

chopped fresh tarragon, to garnish

TO SERVE

freshly cooked rice

mixed salad

Put the wine, vinegar, olive oil, and garlic into a large bowl, and mix until well combined. Season with salt and pepper to taste.

Rinse the tuna steaks under cold running water and pat dry with paper towels. Cut them into small cubes. Wipe the mushrooms clean with paper towels. Thread the tuna cubes onto skewers, alternating them with the mushrooms. When the skewers are full (leave a small space at either end), transfer them to the bowl and turn them in the wine mixture until they are well coated. Cover with plastic wrap and place in the refrigerator to marinate for at least 30 minutes.

Grill the skewers over hot coals for about 10 minutes or until the tuna is cooked right through (but do not overcook), turning them frequently and basting with the remaining marinade. Arrange the skewers on a bed of rice, garnish with chopped fresh tarragon, and serve with a mixed salad.

asian shrimp skewers

very easy

serves 4

15 minutes
+ 2 hours to
marinate

4–5 minutes

ingredients

MARINADE
scant ½ cup vegetable oil
2 tbsp chili oil
scant ¼ cup lemon juice
1 tbsp rice wine or sherry
2 scallions, trimmed and
    finely chopped
2 garlic cloves, finely chopped
1 tbsp grated fresh root ginger
1 tbsp chopped fresh lemongrass
2 tbsp chopped fresh cilantro
salt and pepper

SKEWERS
2 lb 4 oz/1 kg jumbo shrimp, peeled and
    deveined, but with tails left on

GARNISH
wedges of lemon
chopped fresh chives
freshly cooked jasmine rice, to serve

Put the oils, lemon juice, rice wine, scallions, garlic, ginger, lemongrass, and cilantro into a food processor and season well with salt and pepper. Process until smooth, then transfer to a nonmetallic (glass or ceramic) bowl, which will not react with acid.

Add the shrimp to the bowl and turn them in the mixture until they are well coated. Cover with plastic wrap and place in the refrigerator to marinate for at least 2 hours.

When the shrimp are thoroughly marinated, lift them out and thread them onto skewers leaving a small space at either end. Grill them over hot coals for 4–5 minutes or until cooked right through (but do not overcook), turning them frequently and basting with the remaining marinade. Arrange the skewers on a bed of freshly cooked jasmine rice, garnish with lemon wedges and chopped fresh chives, and serve.

shrimp & bell pepper kabobs

very easy   serves 4

15 minutes   4–5 minutes
+ 3–4 hours
to marinate

ingredients

MARINADE

2 scallions, trimmed and chopped
2 garlic cloves, finely chopped
1 green chili and 1 small red chili,
   seeded and finely chopped
1 tbsp grated fresh root ginger
1 tbsp chopped fresh chives
4 tbsp lime juice
1 tbsp finely grated lime zest
2 tbsp chili oil
salt and pepper

KABOBS

24 jumbo shrimp, peeled and deveined,
   but with tails left on
2 bell peppers, 1 red and 1 green,
   seeded and cut into small chunks

GARNISH

wedges of lime
freshly cooked rice or Napa cabbage,
   to serve

Put the scallions, garlic, chilies, ginger, chives, lime juice, lime zest, and chili oil into a food processor and season well with salt and pepper. Process until smooth, then transfer to a nonmetallic (glass or ceramic) bowl, which will not react with acid.

Thread the shrimp onto skewers, alternating them with the red and green bell pepper chunks. When the skewers are full (leave a small space at either end), transfer them to the bowl and turn them in the mixture until they are well coated. Cover with plastic wrap and place in the refrigerator to marinate for 3–4 hours.

Grill the kabobs over hot coals for 4–5 minutes or until the shrimp are cooked right through (but do not overcook), turning them frequently and basting with the remaining marinade. Arrange the skewers on a bed of rice or Napa cabbage, garnish with lime wedges and chopped fresh chives, and serve.

sweet & sour polynesian shrimp

extremely easy

serves 4

5 minutes

8–10 minutes

SAUCE
10½ oz/300 g canned pineapple chunks
scant ¼ cup soy sauce
2 tbsp sweet sherry
3 tbsp red wine vinegar
¼ cup brown sugar

KABOBS
6 strips smoked lean bacon
8 oz/225 g jumbo shrimp, peeled and
    deveined, tails removed
2 bell peppers, 1 red and 1 orange, seeded
    and cut into small chunks
freshly boiled rice, to serve

To make the sauce, drain the pineapple chunks and reserve the juice. Set the pineapple chunks aside for the kabobs. In a separate large bowl, mix together the soy sauce, sherry, red wine vinegar, and sugar, then stir in the reserved pineapple juice.

For the kabobs, cut the bacon strips into small pieces and wrap a piece around each shrimp. Thread the shrimp onto skewers, alternating them with pieces of red and orange bell pepper and the reserved pineapple chunks. When the skewers are full (leave a small space at either end), transfer them to the large bowl and turn them in the mixture until they are well coated.

Grill the kabobs over hot coals for 8–10 minutes or until the shrimp are cooked right through (but do not overcook), turning them frequently and brushing with more sauce as necessary. Arrange the kabobs on a bed of freshly cooked rice and serve.

Vegetarian cooking has really come into its own in recent years, and what better way to celebrate its versatility and diversity than on the barbecue grill? There has never been a better time for experimenting with new ingredients and combinations, especially with the ever-widening range of delicious vegetables and fruits now available to us. This chapter provides some mouthwatering vegetarian dishes to tempt your palate, and an exciting selection of salads which make wonderful accompaniments or light meals in themselves.

vegetarian & salads

mycoprotein & mushroom skewers

very easy   serves 4

10 minutes   5 minutes
+ 1 hour to
marinate

ingredients

MARINADE
2 tbsp extra-virgin olive oil
1 tbsp balsamic vinegar
1 garlic clove, finely chopped
salt and pepper

SKEWERS
1 lb 10 oz/750 g mycoprotein pieces, or
    mycoprotein fillets cut into
    small chunks

1 lb/450 g white mushrooms
1 large pear, cored and cut into
    small chunks
wedges of pear, to garnish

TO SERVE
fresh green and red lettuce
fresh crusty bread

Put the oil, vinegar, and garlic into a large bowl. Season with salt and pepper and mix until well combined.

Thread the mycoprotein pieces onto skewers, alternating them with the mushrooms and pear chunks. When the skewers are full (leave a small space at either end), transfer them to the bowl and turn them in the mixture until they are well coated. Cover with plastic wrap and place in the refrigerator to marinate for at least 1 hour.

Grill the skewers over hot coals for about 5 minutes or until the mycoprotein is cooked right through, turning them frequently and basting with the remaining marinade. Arrange the skewers on a bed of fresh green and red lettuce, garnish with wedges of pear, and serve with fresh crusty bread.

bean & vegetable burgers with tomato salsa

very easy   serves 4

15 minutes   10–20
+ 30 minutes minutes
to chill

BURGERS
7 oz/200 g canned garbanzo beans,
   drained and rinsed
7 oz/200 g canned cannellini beans,
   drained and rinsed
1 large zucchini, finely grated
1 large carrot, peeled and finely grated
1 garlic clove, peeled and finely chopped
3 oz/75 g bread crumbs
salt and pepper

SALSA
4 large tomatoes, chopped
1 tbsp lime juice
2 shallots, peeled and chopped
1 garlic clove, peeled and chopped
1 tbsp chopped fresh basil

GARNISH
chopped fresh basil
wedges of lime
hamburger buns, to serve

Put the garbanzo beans and cannellini beans into a food processor and blend together briefly. Transfer to a large bowl, then add the zucchini, carrot, garlic, and bread crumbs. Season with salt and pepper, then mix together until thoroughly combined. Using your hands, form the mixture into burger shapes, transfer to a shallow dish, and cover with plastic wrap. Refrigerate for 30 minutes.

To make the salsa, put the tomatoes, lime juice, shallots, garlic, and basil into a bowl and stir together. Cover with plastic wrap and set aside.

Grill the burgers over hot coals for 5–10 minutes on each side or until cooked right through. Remove from the coals and transfer to serving plates. Garnish with chopped basil and wedges of lime and serve with hamburger buns and the salsa.

mixed nut burgers with chili

easy   serves 4

25 minutes   10–12
+ 3 hours   minutes
to chill

ingredients

scant ⅔ cup boiling water
2 tbsp soy sauce
7 oz/200 g bulgur wheat
⅔ cup cashews
⅔ cup hazelnuts
⅓ cup almonds
1 garlic clove, grated
1 small red chili, seeded and
    finely chopped

1 tsp dried mixed herbs
1 tbsp tomato paste
4 eggs

TO SERVE
hamburger buns
slices of tomato
chopped mixed nuts, toasted

Pour the boiling water and soy sauce into a heatproof bowl. Rinse and drain the bulgur wheat three times, then add it to the bowl and stir into the liquid. Let stand for 15–20 minutes, or until all the liquid has been absorbed.

While the bulgur wheat is soaking, grind the cashews, hazelnuts, and almonds in a food processor. When the bulgur wheat is ready (and all the liquid has been absorbed), add the ground nuts to the bowl and stir them in. Then add the garlic, chili, mixed herbs, tomato paste, and eggs, and mix until well combined. Cover with plastic wrap and refrigerate for 3 hours.

When the mixture has chilled, form it into burger shapes, then grill over hot coals for 10–12 minutes or until cooked through, turning once. About halfway through the cooking time, add the tomato slices. Cook for 4–5 minutes, turning once. Serve at once with hamburger buns, the tomato slices, and toasted chopped nuts.

stuffed tortillas

easy   serves 4

10–15   15–17
minutes   minutes

ingredients

2 red bell peppers, seeded and
  cut into quarters
4 vegetarian sausages
11½ oz/325 g canned red kidney beans,
  drained, rinsed, and drained again
4 large tomatoes, chopped
1 large onion, chopped
1 garlic clove, chopped
1 tbsp lime juice

1 tbsp chopped fresh basil
salt and pepper
4 large wheat or corn tortillas,
  or 8 small ones

TO SERVE
shredded lettuce
slices of fresh tomato
sour cream

Cook the red bell peppers on the barbecue grill, skin side down, for about 5 minutes or until the skins are blackened and charred. Transfer them to a plastic bag, seal the bag, and set aside.

Grill the sausages over hot coals for 10–12 minutes or until cooked right through, turning them occasionally. While the sausages are cooking, put the kidney beans, tomatoes, onion, garlic, lime juice, and basil into a large bowl. Season with salt and pepper and mix until well combined.

Take the bell pepper quarters from the plastic bag and remove the skins. Chop the flesh into small pieces and add it to the kidney bean mixture. About one minute before the sausages are ready, warm the tortillas on the grill for a few seconds.

Remove the sausages from the grill and cut them into slices. Fill the tortillas with sausage slices, kidney bean salsa, shredded lettuce, tomato slices, and sour cream. Serve at once.

haloumi cheese & vegetable kabobs

very easy   serves 4

10 minutes   5–10
+ 2 hours to   minutes
marinate

ingredients

MARINADE
4 tbsp extra-virgin olive oil
2 tbsp balsamic vinegar
2 garlic cloves, finely chopped
1 tbsp chopped fresh cilantro
salt and pepper

KABOBS
8 oz/225 g haloumi cheese
12 white mushrooms

8 pearl onions
12 cherry tomatoes
2 zucchini, cut into small chunks
1 red bell pepper, seeded and cut
   into small chunks
chopped fresh cilantro, to garnish

TO SERVE
freshly cooked rice or fresh salad greens
fresh crusty bread

Put the oil, vinegar, garlic, and cilantro into a large bowl. Season with salt and pepper and mix until well combined.

Cut the haloumi cheese into bite-size cubes. Thread the cubes onto skewers, alternating them with whole white mushrooms, pearl onions, cherry tomatoes, and zucchini and red bell pepper chunks. When the skewers are full (leave a small space at either end), transfer them to the bowl and turn them in the mixture until they are well coated. Cover with plastic wrap and place in the refrigerator to marinate for at least 2 hours.

When the skewers are thoroughly marinated, grill them over hot coals for 5–10 minutes or until they are cooked to your taste, turning them frequently and basting with the remaining marinade. Arrange the skewers on a bed of freshly cooked rice or fresh mixed salad greens, garnish with cilantro leaves, and serve with fresh crusty bread.

chili beanburgers with onion salsa

easy   serves 4

15–20 minutes   10–20 minutes

ingredients

SALSA
4 large tomatoes, chopped
1 red onion, finely chopped
1 garlic clove, chopped
1 tbsp chopped fresh cilantro
1 tbsp chopped fresh flatleaf parsley
1 tbsp red wine vinegar
1 tbsp lime juice
salt and pepper

BURGERS
8 oz/225 g canned red kidney beans
1 large carrot, boiled and mashed
1 large red onion, finely chopped
½ cup fresh bread crumbs
4 tbsp all-purpose flour
1 tbsp tomato paste
sprigs of fresh cilantro and
   wedges of lime, to garnish

hamburger buns and vegetarian cheese
   slices, to serve

To make the salsa, put the tomatoes, onion, garlic, herbs, vinegar, and lime juice into a bowl. Season with salt and pepper and mix until well combined. Cover with plastic wrap and set aside.

To make the burgers, drain the canned kidney beans, rinse them, and drain them again. Put them into a large mixing bowl with the carrot, onion, bread crumbs, flour, and tomato paste, and mix until well combined. Season well with salt and pepper. Using your hands, form the mixture into burger shapes. Grill the burgers over hot coals for 5–10 minutes on each side or until cooked right through. Garnish with sprigs of fresh cilantro and wedges of lime, and serve with hamburger buns and cheese slices.

cheese & vegetable rolls

easy   serves 4

15 minutes   10 minutes

ingredients

2 red bell peppers, seeded and
   cut into quarters
2 zucchini, trimmed and sliced
1 large onion, cut into rings
5½ oz/150 g baby corn
3 tbsp olive oil

4 large white or whole-wheat rolls,
   cut in half horizontally to make
   8 thinner rounds
4 oz/115 g smoked (cured) semifirm
   cheese, grated
4 tbsp sour cream

Cook the bell peppers on the barbecue grill, skin side down, for 5 minutes or until the skins are charred. Transfer them to a plastic bag, seal it, and set aside. Brush the zucchini, onion rings, and corn with oil, and grill over hot coals for 5 minutes, turning them frequently and basting with more oil if necessary.

While the vegetables are grilling, take the bottom halves of the bread rolls, brush the cut sides with oil, sprinkle over some cheese, and cover with the top halves. Wrap each roll in aluminum foil and transfer them to the grill. Warm for 2–4 minutes, just until the cheese starts to melt (do not overcook).

While the rolls are warming, take the bell pepper quarters from the bag and remove the skins. Chop the flesh into small pieces and transfer it to a plate with the other vegetables.

Transfer the rolls to serving plates and remove the foil. Fill them with the cooked vegetables and sour cream and serve at once.

spicy vegetarian sausages

easy

serves 4

15 minutes
+ 45 minutes
to chill

15 minutes

ingredients

1 garlic clove, finely chopped

1 onion, finely chopped

1 red chili, seeded and finely chopped

14 oz/400 g canned red kidney beans, rinsed, drained, and mashed

2 cups fresh bread crumbs

⅓ cup almonds, toasted and ground

1¾ oz/50 g cooked rice

½ cup grated colby cheese

1 egg yolk

1 tbsp chopped fresh oregano

flour, for dusting

salt and pepper

vegetable oil, for brushing

TO SERVE

fresh bread rolls

sliced onion, lightly cooked

sliced tomato, lightly cooked

tomato catsup and/or mustard

Put the garlic, onion, chili, mashed kidney beans, bread crumbs, almonds, rice, and cheese into a large bowl. Stir in the egg yolk and oregano, then season with salt and plenty of pepper.

Using your hands, form the mixture into sausage shapes. Roll each sausage in a little flour, then transfer to a bowl, cover with plastic wrap, and refrigerate for 45 minutes.

Brush a piece of aluminum foil with oil, then put the sausages on the foil and brush them with a little more vegetable oil. Transfer the sausages and foil to the barbecue grill. Grill over hot coals, turning the sausages frequently, for about 15 minutes or until cooked right through. Serve with bread rolls, cooked sliced onion and tomato, and tomato catsup and/or mustard.

carrot, cabbage & mixed fruit salad

extremely easy

serves 4

10 minutes

7 oz/200 g raw carrots
7 oz/200 g raw white cabbage
3 ½ oz/100 g sprouting beans
1 ¾ oz/50 g alfalfa sprouts
generous ⅓ cup golden raisins
generous ⅓ cup raisins
1 tbsp lemon juice

Trim and peel the carrots, then grate them into a large salad bowl. Trim the white cabbage, then shred it finely. Transfer it to a large strainer and rinse under cold running water. Drain well, then add it to the carrots.

Put the sprouting beans and alfalfa into the strainer and rinse well, then drain and add to the salad. Rinse and drain all the fruit and then add it to the bowl. Pour in the lemon juice, toss the salad in it, and serve.

beet, apple & celery salad

extremely
easy

serves 4

5–10
minutes

i n g r e d i e n t s

i n g r e d i e n t s

2 apples
2 large or 4 small cooked beets
2 celery stalks
scant ½ cup plain yogurt
1 tbsp lemon juice

Wash and core the apples, but leave the skin on. Grate them into a large salad bowl.

Grate the beets, then add them to the bowl with the apples. Wash and trim the celery stalks, cut them into small pieces, then add them to the salad.

Add the yogurt and lemon juice, mix until all the ingredients are thoroughly combined, then serve.

avocado, corn & walnut salad

extremely easy

serves 4

10 minutes

12 oz/350 g canned corn kernels

2¾ oz/75 g walnuts, chopped

2 large, ripe avocados

6 tbsp lemon juice

6 tbsp sour cream

1 oz/25g walnuts,
    chopped, to garnish

Drain the corn kernels, then put them into a large salad bowl. Add the walnuts and mix until well combined.

Peel and pit the avocados, brush them with some of the lemon juice to prevent discoloration, then add them to the salad.

In a separate bowl, mix the remaining lemon juice with the sour cream until a smooth consistency is reached. Add more lemon juice or cream if necessary. Add the lemon cream to the salad, stir it in, and serve.

fava beans with mozzarella & basil

extremely easy

serves 4

10 minutes

5 minutes

ingredients

1 lb/450 g fava beans
  (shelled weight)
4 tbsp extra-virgin olive oil
1 tbsp lime juice
1 tbsp finely chopped fresh basil
2¼ oz/60 g firm mozzarella

GARNISH
finely chopped fresh mint
wedges of lime

Bring a pan of water to a boil, then add the fava beans and cook for 2 minutes. Drain well and let cool.

In a separate bowl, mix together the olive oil, lime juice, and chopped basil.

When the beans are cool, transfer them to a large salad bowl. Pour over the oil dressing and mix until well combined. Cut the mozzarella into cubes and stir them gently into the salad. Garnish with chopped fresh mint and lime wedges and serve.

tabbouleh

extremely easy serves 4

25 minutes 2 minutes

ingredients

7 oz/200 g bulgur wheat
½ cucumber
4 ripe tomatoes
3 scallions
3½ oz/100 g fresh flatleaf parsley
3½ oz/100 g fresh mint
juice of ½ lemon
chopped fresh parsley, to garnish

TO SERVE
4 pitas
wedges of lemon

Rinse and drain the bulgur wheat three times, then transfer it to a large heatproof bowl.

Bring a pot of water to a boil. Pour over enough boiling water to cover the bulgur wheat, with about ½ inch/1 cm more on top. Set aside for 15–20 minutes or until the water has been absorbed.

While the bulgur wheat is soaking, prepare the salad. Peel the cucumber, cut it into small cubes, and transfer it to a large salad bowl. Wash and chop the tomatoes and trim and chop the scallions, then add them to the bowl. Wash and chop the herbs, and add them to the salad with the lemon juice.

When the bulgur wheat is ready, squeeze out any remaining moisture and add it to the salad. Toss the ingredients together and garnish with chopped parsley. Warm the pitas on the barbecue grill for a few seconds, then pass them round with the tabbouleh so that people can stuff them with the salad. Serve with wedges of lemon.

spicy tomato salad

extremely easy

serves 4

5 minutes
+ 10 minutes
to cool

2–4 minutes

ingredients

4 large ripe tomatoes
1 oz/25 g fresh basil
1 small red chili
1 garlic clove
4 tbsp extra-virgin olive oil
1 tbsp lemon juice
2 tbsp balsamic vinegar
salt and pepper

GARNISH
sprigs of fresh basil
wedges of lemon

fresh crusty bread, to serve

Bring a pot of water to a boil. Put the tomatoes into a heatproof bowl, then pour over enough boiling water to cover them. Let them soak for 2–4 minutes, then lift them out of the water and let cool slightly.

When the tomatoes are cool enough to handle, gently pierce the skins with the point of a knife. You should now find the skins easy to remove. Discard the skins, then chop the tomatoes and place them in a large salad bowl.

Seed and finely chop the chili, then chop the garlic. Wash and finely chop the basil, then add it to the tomatoes with the chili and the garlic.

In a separate bowl, mix together the oil, lemon juice, and balsamic vinegar, then season with salt and pepper. Pour the mixture over the salad and toss together well. Garnish with basil sprigs and lemon wedges, and serve with fresh crusty bread.

mixed cabbage coleslaw with fruit

extremely
easy

serves 4

10 minutes

ingredients

3½ oz/100 g white cabbage
3½ oz/100 g red cabbage
2 large carrots
1 onion
1 oz/25 g golden raisins

25 g/1 oz raisins
scant ½ cup mayonnaise
2 tbsp lemon juice
salt and pepper

Wash and shred the white and red cabbage. Grate the carrots, and finely chop the onion. Put all the prepared vegetables into a large salad bowl, then wash the fruit and add to the bowl.

In a separate bowl, mix together the mayonnaise and lemon juice, season with salt and pepper, and pour over the salad. Mix all the ingredients together until well combined. Serve at once, or cover with plastic wrap and refrigerate until ready to use.

potato, arugula & mozzarella salad

very easy   serves 4

10 minutes   15–20
             minutes

ingredients

1 lb 7 oz/650 g small new potatoes
4½ oz/125 g arugula
5½ oz/150 g firm mozzarella
1 large pear
1 tbsp lemon juice
salt and pepper

DRESSING
3 tbsp extra-virgin olive oil
1½ tbsp white wine vinegar
1 tsp sugar
pinch of mustard powder

Bring a pan of salted water to a boil. Add the potatoes, lower the heat, and cook for about 15 minutes, until tender. Remove from the heat, drain, and let cool.

When the potatoes are cool, cut them in half and place them in a large salad bowl. Wash and drain the arugula, cut the mozzarella into cubes, and wash, trim, and slice the pear. Add them to the bowl along with the lemon juice. Season with salt and pepper.

To make the dressing, mix together the oil, vinegar, sugar, and mustard powder. Pour the dressing over the salad and toss all the ingredients together until they are well coated. Serve at once.

Grilled desserts are a special treat and provide a satisfying finale to any al fresco meal. Fruits, in particular, are very healthy and nutritious foods, and are delicious cooked over coals. This chapter contains some truly irresistible concoctions: some are light and refreshing and may include unexpected combinations, such as apple and melon kabobs; others are rich and indulgent, such as grilled bananas covered with melting chocolate and a splash of rum. All are very easy and quick to make.

desserts

apple & melon kabobs

very easy   serves 4

5-10   10 minutes
minutes

6 tbsp butter

1–2 tbsp brown sugar

pinch of allspice

½ melon, such as galia or charentais

2 apples

1 tbsp lemon juice

plain yogurt, mascarpone cheese, or
    ice cream, to serve

In a small pan, melt the butter gently over a low heat. Stir in the brown sugar and allspice, then remove from the heat and pour into a large bowl.

Cut the melon flesh into small chunks. Wash and core the apples, and cut into small chunks. Brush the fruit with lemon juice.

Thread the melon chunks onto skewers, alternating with pieces of apple. When the skewers are full (leave a small space at either end), transfer them to the bowl and turn them in the butter mixture until they are well coated.

Grill the kabobs over hot coals, turning them frequently, for about 10 minutes or until they are cooked to your taste. Serve with plain yogurt, mascarpone cheese, or ice cream.

chocolate rum bananas

very easy   serves 4

5 minutes   5–10
             minutes

ingredients

1 tbsp butter

8 oz/225 g semisweet or milk chocolate

4 large bananas

2 tbsp rum

grated nutmeg, to decorate

mascarpone cheese or ice cream,
  to serve

Take four 10-inch/25-cm squares of aluminum foil and brush them with butter.

Cut the chocolate into very small pieces. Make a careful slit lengthwise in the peel of each banana, and open just wide enough to insert the chocolate. Place the chocolate pieces inside the bananas, along their lengths, then close them up.

Wrap each stuffed banana in a square of aluminum foil, then grill them over hot coals for 5–10 minutes, until the chocolate has melted inside the bananas. Remove from the barbecue grill, place the bananas on serving plates, and pour some rum into each banana. Serve at once with mascarpone cheese or ice cream topped with grated nutmeg.

brandied pineapple rings

very easy   serves 4

5 minutes
+ 1–1½
hours to
marinate

10 minutes

1 pineapple, peeled, cored, and
   cut into rings

MARINADE
2 tbsp honey
3 tbsp brandy

2 tsp lemon juice
sprigs of fresh mint, to decorate

For the marinade, put the honey, brandy, and lemon juice into a large, nonmetallic (glass or ceramic) bowl, which will not react with acid. Stir together until well combined. Put the pineapple rings into the bowl and turn them in the mixture until thoroughly coated. Cover with plastic wrap, transfer to the refrigerator, and let marinate for 1–1½ hours.

When the pineapple rings are thoroughly marinated, lift them out and grill them over hot coals for about 10 minutes, turning them frequently and basting with more marinade if necessary.

Remove the pineapple rings from the barbecue grill, arrange them on individual serving plates, and decorate with fresh mint sprigs.

summer fruit nectarines

very easy   serves 4

5 minutes   10–15
minutes

ingredients

4 large nectarines
7 oz/200 g frozen summer fruits
   (such as blueberries and
   raspberries), thawed
3 tbsp lemon juice
3 tbsp honey

mascarpone cheese or ice cream,
   to serve

Cut out eight 7-inch/18-cm squares of aluminum foil. Wash the nectarines, cut them in half, and remove the pits. Place each nectarine half on a square of foil.

Fill each nectarine half with summer fruits, then top each one with 1 teaspoon of lemon juice, then 1 teaspoon of honey.

Close the foil around each nectarine half to make a package, then grill them over hot coals for 10–15 minutes, according to your taste. Remove from the barbecue grill, place the nectarines on serving plates, and serve with mascarpone cheese or ice cream.

stuffed figs

easy   serves 4

10 minutes   10 minutes

ingredients

8 fresh figs
3½ oz/100 g cream cheese
1 tsp powdered cinnamon
3 tbsp brown sugar

sprigs of fresh mint, to decorate

plain yogurt, mascarpone cheese, or
   ice cream, to serve

Cut out eight 7-inch/18-cm squares of aluminum foil. Make a small slit in each fig, then place each fig on a square of foil.

Put the cream cheese in a bowl. Add the cinnamon and stir until well combined. Stuff the inside of each fig with the cinnamon cream cheese, then sprinkle a teaspoon of sugar over each one. Close the foil round each fig to make a package.

Place the packages on the barbecue grill and cook over hot coals, turning them frequently, for about 10 minutes, or until the figs are cooked to your taste. Transfer the figs to serving plates and decorate with fresh mint. Serve at once with plain yogurt, mascarpone cheese, or ice cream.

grilled apples

easy   serves 4

10 minutes   10 minutes

4 apples
3 tbsp lemon juice
3 tbsp butter
4 tsp brown sugar
8 tbsp sweet mincemeat
plain yogurt or mascarpone cheese,
    to serve

Wash the apples, then cut them in half from top to bottom. Remove the cores and seeds, then brush the cut sides of the apples with lemon juice to prevent discoloration.

Put the butter in a small pan and gently melt it over a low heat. Remove from the heat, then brush the cut sides of the apples with half of the butter. Reserve the rest of the melted butter.

Sprinkle the apples with sugar, then transfer them to the barbecue grill, cut sides down, and cook over hot coals for about 5 minutes. Brush the apples with the remaining butter, then turn them over. Add a tablespoon of mincemeat to the center of each apple, then cook for another 5 minutes, or until they are cooked to your taste.

Remove from the heat and transfer to serving plates. Serve at once with plain yogurt or mascarpone cheese.

index